100 COMMANDMENTS

- For The -
Millennial Entrepreneur

Key Principles Every Business Owner Should Follow

Written By:

TERESA SAFFOLD

Copyright © 2018 by Teresa Saffold.

All rights reserved. No part of this book may be used or reproduced by any means, graphic, electronic, or mechanical, including photocopying, recording, taping, or by any information storage retrieval system, without the written permission of the publisher except in the case of brief quotations embodied in critical articles and reviews.

Table of Contents

Acknowledgments 1

Introduction 3

Chapter One: Commandments Of Great Leadership 6

Chapter Two: Commandments Of Savvy Marketing And Promotion 15

Chapter Three: Commandments Of World Class Client Service 26

Chapter Four: Commandments Of Mastering Sales 35

Chapter Five: Commandments Of Sound Finances 44

Chapter Six: Commandments Of Effortless Operations 50

Chapter Seven: Commandments Of A Success Mindset 59

Acknowledgments

In life there is nothing like having support to be able to carry out your passionate purpose. This book although written by one individual took a team of so many others to carry the vision. Thank you to all of the torch carriers along the way that reinforced my potential that this book was possible. To my family that thinks the world of me and my literary talents, to my children, Lydia and Amaree who inspire me to get better because they reflect their inspiration back to me through following in my footsteps. To my husband Chris who makes sure I am always afforded the time off from mom duties to live my dreams and speak positive affirmations over my life. A special thank you to my father, Edward who shows me how proud he is of my accomplishments, and keeps the fire raging in me to keep making Daddy proud. To my late mother, Teresa who taught me everything I know about how to communicate. Mom, if it had not been for your rearing me in effective communication skills, I cannot say I would be here today. To my whole Power BAR Women's Fitness team family that supports me when it is hard, celebrates with me when it is easy, and have been my willing students to be coached by this book's principles.

There are so many others who supported, encouraged, mentored, guided, and prayed for me that it would take a whole other book to mention. I truly appreciate the seeds so many have sown into my life. The deep human desire to make others happy with whom we are can go a very long way, particularly when you are blessed with those that are not too proud, jealous, or insecure to share with you how proud they truly are. I hope that with this book you are even more proud of your investment into my life so that we may continue this journey of life's fulfillment together as friends and family.

Introduction

I remember like it was yesterday, the stomach dropping feeling as if I had just started to descend at an unimaginable rate of high velocity speed to drop off the World's tallest rollercoaster falling straight into a deep plunge of twists and turns and upside down maneuvers. I was screaming on the inside and numb on the outside. What the hell did I just sign up for? Who was I kidding? I had no business degree, I have a family I help support, I already have a 10 year career that I know like the back of my hand and I am risking it all for business ownership!

What did I know about business, entrepreneurship, balance sheets, and business plans anyways? Did I just make the biggest and most detrimental mistake of my life? You would think that after procrastinating for more than 14 years to finally go into business for myself full time I would be better prepared for this decision right? More capital for cushion, a big well thought out business plan put together by the most prestigious lawyer in town all wrapped up with a bow on it.

I could hear the fears in my conscious remembering the main reason why I never did take that move to go into business for myself as an all in entrepreneur and suddenly my confidence was taking hit after hit and the negativity was swelling quickly.

Then I began to do something that would be the onset of all the success I would have over the following years to come. This one key element helped me to continue to establish principles that would guide me through decisions, redirections, and pivots in my business, innovations, and leadership. There was one task that had to be done full on in order for me not to sink, but rather swim, and for me to discover the confidence necessary to thrive. That one thing, that one task, that one single handed principle that I discovered was nothing new under the sun, but is so often overlooked – especially for this fast paced millennial filled society of entrepreneurs. This one thing was to Read and Study and become an ongoing learner of business.

Yep, study. You see, as a once called, "Work Horse" I believed that business success was primarily brought on by performing massive amounts of grunt work, staying in constant motion, #TeamNoSleep, and the ultimate hustle where you can wear your sagging bags under your eyes like trophies. It took almost a year for me to finally heed the advice of one of my mentors to read for a measly 15 minutes a day and absorb some helpful information that may just change my business for the better. Why was I so restless and never willing to take the time to learn in the beginning I thought? Well, it wasn't really hustling that I was doing as I had convinced myself, it was operation panic.

Sheer utter panic that I had to spend every waking hour grinding to make it because my entire lively hood was centered on this business now, but what I didn't know was you have to take the time to sharpen your axe. I also didn't discover until later that there are trends in success where the basic principles do not change no matter what the business is. These principles were collected over various circumstances, from different successful mentors, and throughout my readings and analyzation of entrepreneurship. All of my teachings and how they influence me and others have been written for you in "100 Commandments for the Millennial Entrepreneur" so that you can visit the chapters to find your center when you need some guidance. These writings are not just for the millennial entrepreneur, but for any business owner to recap the basic principles of running a successful organization. This book and I wish you much success on your journey and venture. I hope you enjoy this read.

CHAPTER ONE

Commandments of Great Leadership

1. ***Thou shall value your staff – even if it is a staff of one.*** Your staff can bury your vision and make a muck of you as a leader, your business, and your goals. Treating staff poorly by being overtly demanding, condescending, or evasive can reflect poorly on you as a leader. Remember the great and the not so great leaders from your past and emulate the great ones who helped you get to where you are today. Follow the Golden Rule, also known as the Platinum Rule, "Treat others as you would want to be treated". See your staff as an asset, people who you develop and treat with high regard, just as you expect them to treat your clients.

2. ***Thou shall practice ethical business standards.*** Everything done in the dark will surface to the light. Do not make sideline deals or show favoritism to one person you do business with over the next. In banking this would be referred to as the Bank Secrecy Act which protects clients from being treated differently from

their fellow depositors for any reason. If you greet one client with a smile, which I hope you do - then all clients should be greeted with a smile. Of course we know embezzlement and fraud are out of the question under this commandment! Practice moral business standards with clients and staff at all times, because integrity will always prevail.

3. ***Thou shall have clean ears to hear, listening more than you speak.*** Remember you are not really listening when you are talking – even if this talking is being done internally. Never become so smart that you devalue other people's input. This can be difficult in times where you really believe you are the expert in a certain subject manner and a fresh face decides to lecture you on the right way to go about a certain topic, however there may be a new way of doing something they can share. Remember that you can learn from everyone, even if the advice is not usable you can learn what not to do. Always listen more than you talk, for in the listening to your staff you are displaying your best leadership.

4. ***Thou shall show yourself friendly.*** Happy leadership is the best leadership. Leaders who love those that serve their vision and provide a positive atmosphere to work in help staff thrive. By building genuine rapport with those you employ you will

increase the chances of their primary motivator to work being because they love what they do and the environment in which they do it in, verses just to benefit their financial needs. When staff sees leadership as friendly it heightens the level of trust and communication. They are more inclined to give you feedback about their job satisfaction and what they know about the clients' satisfaction rating of the company. Your friendliness should be genuine and authentic. You should also ensure your friendliness doesn't interfere with your ability to be an authority figure when necessary. There is a balance to maintain in leadership that leads and corrects and motivates and inspires.

5. ***Thou shall not be a one man show.*** Delegate tasks so that your time can be spent as a visionary, and not as an employee. Being free to be the visionary and not the employee will allow you to have a watchful eye over the future of your company and the health of the organization. Most business owners refuse to give up the task driven work out of fear that an employee will make too many mistakes. If you find a faithful person who can perform at least 80% of the work as good as you can, give them the repetitive task driven assignments and go create. Your forward movement and protection over what you have already built in the company will only come from having the freedom

to study the market and strategic planning. Overloading on task driven work can serve as a stunt to your growth because you are not in tuned with what's new or changing in your industry. Don't fall into the trap of working in your business and make a commitment to work on your business.

6. ***Thou shall see your staff as assets and not liabilities.*** Your staff allows you to stay in business and keep the doors of your operations open, even if they are digital. Invest in your staff as you would any asset and watch the value increase. Provide avenues for them to grow monetarily, feed their need for validation, help them discover their gifts and talents, allow them to cultivate their purpose. As a word of caution, ensure the assets you choose to employ do not have a depreciating character and will also bring value to your company as they began to be invested in.

7. ***Thou shall be a known and present force in your Company.*** Always be a visible presence in your company so that the staff knows you are fully engaged with your brand. Do not grow so big that you believe it to be unimportant to check in on the work that your staff is producing as bad habits and employees can grow to become cancers that you cannot cure if left untreated. If you do not have the appropriate staff to monitor

activities that do not align with your mission and correct them quickly, being an absentee business owner can be working against you to the point of business failure. Make sure to schedule regular checkups with all of your staff and allow them to hear from you often.

8. ***Thou shall be an inspiration.*** As a leader you should be something that people desire to emulate and that they admire. There should be a fire in you that is bigger than all of your organization and is highly contagious. The people within your organization should feel reignited with inspiration when they leave a meeting with you and should want to go out and do even more of what it takes to be successful at whatever it is your company promotes, as well as important personal goals of their own. Commit to being a trail blazer leader.

9. ***Thou shall be proactive and not reactive.*** This will come from planning in the quiet times so that you are prepared in the turbulence. Meet with your team often to discuss ways that your operations can become more streamlined and efficient. Find out from them what struggles they have been dealing with and look for the common fix. Most of your team may not approach you when things are going wrong until it almost becomes too late. They may assume you are too busy and cannot handle another

issue; they may want to try and handle it on their own so that they can prove their competency, or they may just not be engaged enough to care. By having regular communications you can stay ahead of your team's dilemmas and equip your staff to handle issues as they arise, which will also aid in their feelings of empowerment.

10. ***Thou shall understand your teams' motivations.*** All staff is not created equal. You must get to know those you lead to better understand what motivates them. People skills are essential in the game of business as they either thrust you into success or stand in the way of it. Getting to know others and the truth behind what they want can propel you to the number one spot of leadership in the eyes of your staff. Speaking to the motivation that is specific to each of your staff members is critical and can truly work in your favor and the teams favor when everyone feels they are understood and are being served. Discover the 6 basic human needs that everyone has to better help you identity each member of your staff's true objective.

11. ***Thou shall vet vehemently.*** When you are a rising success story others will see this before you do. This makes you prey to the industry thieves who seek out unbeknowning mentors that they intend to copy all of the intellectual information from. Be sure

to vet out everyone around you intently and thoroughly to ensure they are not in possession of ill ulterior motives. Set up specific personality tests that will pair up your needs, strengths, and weaknesses with theirs. Seek out their background and investigate their goals. Know what type of people may not be suitable to be get close to your internal intellectual property and understand the key traits of loyalty that are easily identifiable to you and your hiring managers. Trust can be hard to come by in business as there are a lot of manipulative people who will attempt to infiltrate your already made system so that they can steal your trade secrets rather than go create for themselves. Become very savvy in identifying who these people may be, how they may position themselves, and what channels you will investigate to see if they could be loyal staff.

12. ***Thou shall be fast to fire and slow to hire.*** Allowing cancerous staff into your company can mean death to your business. Although tough at times, a true leader is able to protect the fort by any means necessary. Being a leader is about seeking the good for all and understanding how one person's actions can affect the moral of everyone else. Your team is watching how you deal with a bad hire and not firing them quickly will reflect poorly on you. Slowly choose those you allow into your company and

set up an organized hiring process to ensure you have a steady pipeline of candidates and never have to make a rash hiring decision that could be costly in the end. Create a vetting system that will allow you and your hiring staff to identify the most important elements needed in a person that will add value to the company and how you can cross pollinate each of your needs. If the candidate cannot complete all phases of your hiring process – and there should be a process, then you have probably saved yourself the bad guy badge of needing to fire them in the first place.

13. *Thou shall believe the best in those you employ.* Being a leader can become frustrating as you are vivaciously passionate about your vision and end goal and others just don't seem to share in the same frequency of the excitement all the time. Employees are often not able to see what hasn't come to fruition yet in the same capacity as you, which can leave you completely flustered and accusatory of them that they may not care about the success of the company. The truth is, almost all of your employees will want to see the company succeed because it directly benefits them when the company thrives. You will need to practice high levels of emotional intelligence understanding that they were not given the vision – you were, therefore they may appear to be

negligent, passive, nonchalant, and disengaged even when they think they are serving the company well. What if they just haven't been provided a clear enough vision to understand what they should really be doing? What if they are truly trying as hard as their skillsets will take them? It is up to you to constantly remember that you will see the success first, as well as the needs. As a leader, you will be responsible in communicating to your team in ways they understand to foster the engagement you really want. Their performance whether good or bad is really the responsibility of the leader. What you experience from your staff is a direct result of the hiring decisions, vetting system, company standards and mission statements, and the preset expectations given to them upon hire. Believing the best in your staff, means you also believe the best in your hiring system.

CHAPTER TWO

Commandments of Savvy Marketing and Promotion

14. ***Thou shall not steal competitor's content.*** The quickest way to sink your business ship is to steal competitor's content and use it as your own. The act of copying is really saying there is a shortage in understanding. It's as if you were back in grade school and that one kid in the classroom didn't study for the test. They had no understanding of the information being asked and they stretched their eyes across the table to simply fill in the blanks on their paper so they wouldn't get a failing grade. When you can create and market your own ideas it gives proof that you understand your industry, your clients' needs and wants, and know how to communicate it to them. Your competitor has their own DNA in business with a specific market, unique style, and a budget specific to their cash flows. Do not attempt to wear another business owner's shoes. Spend the time, energy, and financial resources to develop your own marketing strategy that

will speak to your uniqueness as a company. There are many free resources out today from marketing journals, YouTube videos, podcasts, and local free marketing events you can become a part of to learn. You are in business to be different, not a #metoo.

15. ***Thou shall seek out trends.*** Keeping a watchful eye on your industry can be very exciting and enlightening. When in business, particularly a business you absolutely love you can become engulfed with your own perception of what you sell. In actuality however, the industry you are in could be taking a major turn into a direction you couldn't see coming through your love lenses. Staying logical by watching the trends of your industry will allow you to stay alert and give you the flexibility to adjust so that your bottom line doesn't take a hit. For example, trends help you identify busier seasons, if something in the news caused a spike of attention to your industry, if an indirect competitor is beginning to dominate your market, and allows you to forecast future success or declines. There are different trend tools available, but Google has a free resource you can take advantage of to stay ahead.

16. ***Thou shall not give up full control over your marketing.*** Your marketing is your brand and your brand is how people identify

whether or not they will do business with you. Your messages should always be approved by you to ensure the message fosters the reputation you want to have. Don't be like some of those famous, well established brands who were forced into public backlash for putting out offensive or ill represented marketing messages, sparking the company to take a seat in the humility chair and offer worldwide public apologies. It is okay to hire marketing companies to handle this very important task, but as a leader of your brand you are responsible for your business reputation. Once a good name is damaged, it can be very difficult to recover in the eyes of consumers. It's always best to have a say in the content shared with your target market and understand the impact it will have on them.

17. ***Thou shall innovate regularly.*** Thieves come to steal, kill, and destroy. Copy Cats steal valuable ideas thus killing the profits of the business as the ability to be an exclusive provider is destroyed. Without innovation you have nothing to continue with therefore the only ideas you possessed become annihilated in the marketplace. Be sure you are constantly perfecting your company by renovating old ways of doing things and innovating new and exciting products or services for your targeted market.

Consumers always want what's new and improved. The latest update could save you from a liquidation sale.

18. ***Thou shall have a documented yearly marketing plan.*** As the Sea has a rising tide so does the waves of creativity. Be sure to preserve the highest points of your creative genius with a written marketing plan and fine tune it throughout the year. Spend time planning for the growth of your company and understand what your markets high points are. What do they celebrate the most? When are they most active in purchasing? What excites them? Your marketing plan will allow you to prepare for the variations of purchasing throughout the year and be overly prepared to exceed your clients' expectations. You can create different events, promotions, and sales and fine tune the budgeting to ensure max return. Marketing plans allow you time to secure the best vendors, do product research, and reach more people than you could with last minute planning. Your marketing plan could always change, but at least you will have a guide to follow if nothing else. Have something drafted for each month at a minimum.

19. ***Thou shall have at least three marketing platforms.*** Having multiple platforms of marketing is not just to reach more people, but to make sure you stay relevant if one of the platforms

crashes. If you have been in business any amount of time you may have heard the term algorithm passed around. This is how platforms such as Google and Facebook determine what their users see and why. These change quite frequently to make sure that savvy marketers are putting out useable content people are really searching for in an ethical manner. The change of an algorithm on any platform in which you have built up a major following can drastically decrease your business almost overnight. It may also take days, weeks, and months to learn the new requirements for the platform so that you may rank. This is why having at least three platforms where your company is popular on will benefit you. If one crashes you have back up. You are then able to work on reestablishing the fallen platform while the other two perform as they always have and bring in the cash flow.

20. *Thou shall not give up complete control of your website.* Unless you are in the information technology industry, your website can be a total nightmare. Your website is the heartbeat of your business in this online age. This is how consumers find you and buy from you, and if you don't have an online presence you are missing a major amount of money to be made. This is why companies pay thousands of dollars to land their brand name in

the top 5 spots of Google because research has shown that those on the top of the first page of Google gain the most business. There is a lot more to loading a website with great design and eye catching content such as SEO (search engine optimization) and back end coding that may require the expertise of professional website developers. When hiring someone to work on your website it is highly advised that you refrain from giving up complete admin control over your site. There have been instances in which website developers will lock the owner of companies out of their websites and pretty much hijack their website and all its success.

This can be crucially devastating to you as a business, especially if the website was already ranking and driving traffic that converted into dollars for you. Giving partial access is okay, but don't trust the entire website to someone else. In addition, always have a final say in the esthetics of the website. Writing code and graphic designers are two different talents, and your website can be ranking sky high because of the written content but the colors, designs, photos drive people away from your business because it is poorly styled. Be true to your brand and your targeted market and be very diligent on maintaining control over this area of your company. Keep in mind the importance of your website as your digital finger print and keep it safe.

21. ***Thou shall be easy to do business with.*** People spend money on things that they need, that bring comfort, or make them happy. In essence people pay others to make their lives simpler. So why make it hard for people to do business with you with complex rules and lengthy processes that disengage the end user? The easier it is for people to do business with you, the more sales you will make. Limit the amount of controlling processes you have that stop people from the enjoyment of the process they get from shopping. Do an in depth analysis of your processes and procedures, restrictions and rules and determine if there are some that can be lumped together to make the fine print shorter on your marketing. Be there when your target market needs you, have the proper resources for them to use when they have questions, and anticipate where your target market may get confused about your product and do a great job at writing easy to read content for your website or social media pages that will answer those questions up front. The easier you are to do business with the more trust people will have in your company, lessening the fear that they are going to be bamboozled.

22. ***Thou shall keep it simple.*** Simplicity is the key to success. Similar to the above commandment, simplicity builds trust. The brain can only recognize things in patterns of threes. When we overload the brain, panic and doubt set in on your buyer who either move on to your competition to shop with them or they do nothing with you. This is obviously a result you do not want. Confused buyers become fearful of what they are purchasing because there is so much information being thrown at them they are not sure if they are making the right decision. Before you can get savvy buyers, you must first become a savvy marketer. The key for you to stay simple is to know the one thing you will be targeting, the one question you will answering, or the one problem you are attempting to solve for your clients and speak to that in the offer. Keep in mind, you can have several different offers to advertise, but they should not bleed in the other offers. Do not be afraid to be simple. Do not be afraid to be hyper targeted and speak to only one topic. Wanting to be all things to all people cause business owners to be overly complex and do the opposite of what buyers react to. Always remember to K.I.S.S. *(Keep it simple savvy)*

23. ***Thou shall be a story teller.*** People do not buy features, and they have started to stop buying benefits, people buy purpose. In this

millennial age consumers want to connect with the brands they buy from. They want to know you are bigger than the products and services you are selling and they want to get behind causes that resonate with them. Whether you are a lawyer or a chef, answer the WHY for your market. Tell your story of how the brand came about to your targeted market that compels them to shop with you. Your reasoning should be truthful, no *Milli Vanilli* business allowed! Put your story up on the website, in the locations, in inserts of online purchases, but allow your story to be heard and seen. Allow your company to be transparent and help people feel like when they purchase from you they are contributing to a greater cause. It's a great time to be in business, because you can truly follow your passion and not the dollar as this is what the consumers are seeking more of today.

24. ***Thou shall be seen.*** Money follows Attention. What does this mean? It means getting attention is the only reason to market. Marketing is about getting the most market attention and being so creative and entertaining you keep it. In order to do this, you must go with the demands of the market and follow how they communicate. If your market research proves that they respond best in face to face scenarios then your face should be in every place you can possibly be seen in. Some products or services sell

the most online through stores such as Amazon or Shopify, and others sell the most doing Tutorial Styled Marketing like You Tube and Facebook Feeds. Just get out there and be seen! Become the spokesperson of your brand and learn public speaking skills that will make you millions. Become comfortable campaigning for your company and being an attention seeker. People cannot do business with you when they don't know you exist.

25. ***Thou shall not attempt to attach yourself to someone else's success.*** When you are new in business it is almost natural for you to want to partner with other booming businesses and hitch a ride on their already booming clientele. This is almost always not a great idea. When starting a new business the fear of failure is at one of its highest points and fear can breed a lot of unwanted reactions such as desperation.

To bring in the business entrepreneurs will find themselves making deals they wouldn't normally do because they need the sales, lowering prices to points they normally would not dare to go to capture a new client, and seeking out other businesses as partners that they haven't fully investigated just to grab the attention of their clientele. When partnering with a business you should also be delivering something valuable to them, which can be quite hard when you are new in business. Be very cautious of partnering with other businesses because your associations can influence the way potential clients perceive you.

In addition, you may find yourself at the mercy of the already established business that will set restrictions on your operations if you have physically partnered with them at their location. Consider your business your baby, whom you wouldn't leave with just anybody to help you raise it. Be sure to thoroughly vet all associations you attach your company to if you are going to partner. You can also just weather the startup storm by seeking out business education on how to overcome start up obstacles and use your creativity to capture resources you need to grow.

CHAPTER THREE

Commandments of World Class Client Service

26. ***Thou shall vow to produce measurable results.*** If producing measurable results for clients is not in your business model than consider your company a placebo business. Your focus for any business, whether product or service should be to add measurable value that no other business in your industry can offer. This is one definite way to ensure you can separate yourself from the #metoo market. By first finding out what the number one problem your targeted market has and how your product or service can solve it. Then you will test out your product or service on your targeted consumer and document their progression. You shouldn't wait for clients to tell you that what you are offering is a dud. You should know who your product or service will work for and who it will not. Cease from marketing to everyone as with all products and services there is no one size fits all. The only way to know if you can promise

your clients measurable results is by tracking numerical data through client usage and satisfaction ratings. Then use those satisfaction ratings to steer you in continually offering measurable results to your market.

27. ***Thou shall honor the ground the clients walk on.*** Chivalry in business should never die. Clients make it possible for you to stay in business whether it is Business to Business or public transactions. When your focus is solely on sales, your brand, your achievements, and all about your company it is guaranteed that you have turned a deaf ear to your clients' desires and needs. You must be willing to wow the customer through your service before, during, and after the transactions have taken place. Go above and beyond what you market to your clients. Don't be a one night stand in business. Following up with clients allows insight on future company development and will resonate with the clients letting them know you are in business for the right reasons – service. Your number one goal is to set such an impression of client care that you have clients for life....who bring more clients for life.

28. ***Thou shall expect and practice excellence.*** It is the details that matter. When developing a team and managing operations check all the details. Examine all of the client touch points and

seek out ways where improvements can be made. To go really far in business it requires you to go into the trenches of your offerings and tie bows around all the processes and procedures. Clients may never say that they notice the small details, but they definitely do. Think about your experiences as a consumer where you can tell that the company has really paid attention to the end user experience verses one who simply goes through the obvious motions. Which one would you be most likely to recommend? Which one would you most likely return to? If you will not invest in yourself, why should someone else?

29. ***Thou shall have a public mission statement.*** Today, many consumers want to understand what your end goal is as a business. Did you just set up shop for economic reasons or because you hated your daytime job? What is your driving force for commerce? What do you intend to do with their patronage? Why is this you ask? Because people have a natural need to want to know they are contributing to a cause greater than themselves. When you open up your company and share with the world what you hope to accomplish many clients will appreciate you for being bold in your beliefs and will offer their support and resources to help you attain it. This is why so many

Go Fund Me campaigns work. When people understand the vision they are more apt to actually contribute and follow it.

30. ***Thou shall be responsive.*** One of the number one complaints consumers have is that the businesses they contacted never contacted them back. No call backs, no emails, no returned instant messaging, just purely frustrated clients who want to do business with you. Business is a relationship! What relationship out there is strictly transactional and completely void of communication that turns out happily ever after? With this millennial age and increase in technology the human touch is losing its strength. When consumers do business with a company that is responsive to their needs they feel happier doing business there and trust that they will be well taken care of.

31. ***Thou shall follow up.*** Follow up is King. Where businesses truly thrive is in their follow up plans. For those businesses that are seeking to stay around for the long haul, you must get into the habit of following up with your clients. Do you currently know right now how your clients feel about their relationship with your company? When is the last time you have checked in on them? Follow up is not just for sales generation. Following up is for relationships. It is the phone call your spouse makes to you in the middle of the day to make sure you made it to your

meeting on time or to just hear your voice. Following up like a loving spouse allows you to stay top of mind for your clients and grant them positive reflection about your company. Follow up can be proactive in solving issues you were not made aware of, it allows clients to know they were not forgotten, and it gives room for you to save money on marketing, because it is cheaper to take care of existing clientele than to try and acquire new clients.

32. ***Thou shall reward.*** Make it a habit to find ways to reward your clients for doing business with you. Rewards are positive triggers in the human emotions that make an interaction memorable and create a feeling of happiness. Customers who are regularly recognized by those they do business with are happier and more likely to be loyal and natural ambassadors of your company. The law of reciprocity still works but be sure to maintain a genuine interest in your clients and not just give to get.

33. ***Thou shall be professional.*** No matter how new or inexperienced you are in business, it costs you nothing to learn the art of professionalism. Professionalism is simply manners and business etiquette that allows clients to recognize your value. Small things like the type of background music you play, to the front window being clean, to the usage of the clients name

during a transaction all play critical roles in your levels of perceived professionalism. Clients are not our friends in the regards that we may loosen our top button and get too relaxed with them – in conversation or service. Set a standard in how your company will treat clients and abide by it, whether it is a friend or family member who arrives to do business with you, maintain that standard at all times.

34. *Thou shall know their name.* A person's name is valuable. We take pride in our identity and want others to get it right. When someone forgets our name, it can seem as if we were forgotten in some capacity. If someone refuses to take the time to learn our names correctly we can become defensive, feeling a bit of insignificance in their eyes. This is certainly not what you want from someone you are spending money with on a regular basis with. A business can do everything right, from pricing to service to delivery, but if they refuse to get the repeat customer's name right that client will begin to feel more like a number verses a valued client. Take the time to learn the client's name. Be sure to use their name in every single transaction a minimum of three times. Celebrate their identity as you celebrate when they make a purchase. If you are not good with names, being mindful of using them will make you better.

35. ***Thou shall go the extra mile.*** Don't stop at the end of the purchase. Ask yourself what can I do better or what can I do more of? Doing what is easy is doing what is expected. When you are fully engaged with client service then you will always be looking for opportunities to make a client feel absolutely special. People buy emotionally, and it is always the way you make them feel that will dictate how often and if they ever return to your company. Be sure to give permission to your staff to go the extra mile in service and to use their own creativity to wow the clients you are asking them to serve.

36. ***Thou shall educate them.*** Give a man a fish and he will eat for a day. Teach a man to fish and he will eat for a lifetime. Educate your clients on your product or service and they will be clients for life. Knowledge is empowerment. When people believe they are knowledgeable about something they are almost always ignited with excitement and have an ambitious drive to share their expertise. Why? Because in a sense it makes them look good. When we can teach someone something that is useful and helpful to them we look like the hero, and we feel amazing for the liberation we caused to that person through the knowledge we shared. Being great at what you do is never about how well

you do it, but always about how well you can teach someone else to do it better.

37. ***Thou shall be of clear expectation.*** Communication is vital if you are going to provide a World Class Experience. Never assume your client knows all the details about your processes and procedures and the fine print that comes along with doing business with you. There is always fine print if you are doing business right, because there is always that small percentage of consumers out there hunting for the loop holes in your company to get something for free, so you have to put regulations on how you conduct business. Setting an upfront clear expectation of what you promise to provide, policies such as returns and cancellations, and any guarantees you may have will almost always result in a smoother business and client relationship. Clients may not agree with your policies, but they can respect them if you have done your job at communicating that clearly ahead of time.

38. ***Thou shall be transparent.*** Honesty is truly the best policy. When you attempt to hide important details from clients because you are afraid it will cost you a sale or you withhold information that will be helpful for them to make an educated decision you are not providing world class service. Facades in

business never work, because at some point the client will see the real thing. For example, stock imagery is a no go in building trust with clients. The millennial age consumer wants to see the good, bad, and ugly and stock imagery is a cover up of who your company really is. Infomercials no longer work in these days of business. Clients notice everything! Give your clients the opportunity to see the truth, and keep getting better at what you lack. Clients and future clients will appreciate your transparency and trust your brand more.

39. ***Thou shall right your wrongs.*** There is almost nothing worse than having done business with a company and they weren't able to fully deliver on their product or service and they didn't attempt to try and make it right. Maybe they gave you a faulty product that truly was a fluke, but they made you pay for shipping to send it back. Maybe they mistakenly scheduled you at the wrong time and then asked you to rearrange your schedule, you obliged, and they didn't throw in a little extra for the inconvenience. How a company acts when something goes wrong speaks volumes on their ability to lead in world class service. Inevitably things will go wrong in a transaction or two while in business, but you have to be humble enough to pay for the inconveniences of your clients.

CHAPTER FOUR

Commandments of Mastering Sales

40. ***Thou shall not compete on price.*** Competing on price is the quickest business liquidation you will ever have. Compete on value and not on price. Lowering prices below market level can actually have a crippling effect on your brand as people will see your products and services as defective and cheap. They will be able to spot the desperation in your marketing and question the quality. It can be very tempting to compete on price, because you will feel as if everyone else is winning and you can't make a sale because your products or services are higher in price. This will be the time as an entrepreneur to take a step back and reevaluate what it is you truly deliver. You will have to pull yourself and your team together to discuss how to position the value you provide to those who are interested in doing business with you. If it is something truly valuable and you are not setting your prices at a high ticket amount simply to get rich, then you will be able to find a valid argument as to why your prices are

set at what they are. Every business has a value and the value you provide should match your price tag. If you compete on price you trade in your worth for the value of your competitors and level the playing field until there is no field left.

41. ***Thou shall network with quality people.*** Networking events can be a complete waste of time if you do not choose wisely. With time being such a valuable commodity as an entrepreneur you just cannot waste your time going to everything you are invited to or see on the internet. Some networking events are about how many business cards you can shove in someone's face and how many people you can present your elevator pitch to. Then some other networking events are about the happy hour specials. Choose networking events that put you around a quality group of people, who may have more experience than you, been in business longer, or has prescreened attendees you know would be valuable in connecting with. Do not waste precious time at unstructured networking opportunities and always go with a plan.

42. ***Thou shall be prepared.*** Preparation is the mother of success and with sales this is very true, but even for more than the obvious reasoning. We can all picture the unprepared sales person shoveling around in their paperwork looking for the

latest marketing flyer and recanting their words because they can't seem to remember the exact way to pitch a product or service. We really would be more distracted by their disorganization and lack of preparation than if they were pitching to use free gold. Being prepared in sales is also an excellent way to guard against rebuttals or unexpected price hagglers. When you have a pitch for a product or service spend time alone with it to shoot as many holes in the offer as you possible can. Come up with how many ways can someone try to strike a deal and negotiate you out of your profit. How many excuses can someone actually come up with in your targeted market as to why this isn't for them? Working diligently on not just your pitch, but the aftermath of questions, negotiations, and rebuttals will save a sale more than a nicely campaigned marketing ad.

43. *Thou shall not overcomplicate things.* Keeping sales simple for people to understand allows the potential clients to feel they can trust you and that they are more in control of their buying decision because they understand the offer. When you give a person too much information or not the right information because you didn't ask enough questions your pitch can become gargled and suspicious to a potential buyer. They may fear that

with all you're offering they will be paying for something they don't need. You might hear rebuttals like, "Well, I don't think I will be able to fully take advantage of it." People want the FULL VALUE for their investment. How to avoid overcomplicating a pitch is to ask a ton of questions that direct you to the one major product or service you can offer, then stay there until you have answered every question and hopefully have closed the sale. Additional items can be added on for suggestion after the initial close.

44. ***Thou shall fall in love with sales.*** Sales are not the devil, so stop acting like it. Sales are every human beings way of life. If you want a promotion at a job, if you actually want a job, if you are negotiating with a vendor, if you are wanting someone to give you an opportunity over another, if you are hoping to find true love…life is a big game of sales. It is all about who can pitch the best value. Selling a product or service is about simply offering that product or service to someone you believe would benefit from it. Selling is not being a money shark preying on people who cannot afford the product or service or do not need it. Many people hate the word sales because most have been victim to feeling as if they were finagled out of their hard earned dollars at one point or another in life and have vowed they would never

do anyone else like that. The truth is it is your duty to sale. Sales are a way to help others, especially when you are actually providing value. It is getting someone to invest in themselves in a way that will benefit them, whether happiness, entertainment, health, etc. This is why to love sales – you must be selling something that you believe in or you will never be able to actually fall in love with selling.

45. ***Thou shall be first.*** The early bird absolutely gets the worm. The first in the mind of the prospect will likely be the one to close the sale, and then it is good luck for business number two, three, and four. Always make it a priority to be first to market. When you are first to market you compete with no one, but yourself.

46. ***Thou shall not desire everyone's money.*** All money is not good money. Some money will cost you more money in the long run than the original amount received. Money tied to the sale should match the amount of resources available. This is why overly discounting your products and services could truly attract the wrong market. Quickly identify the types of clients that your business does not want to work with. What are some disqualifiers of great consumers for your product or service that you can think of? Sometimes when you know what you don't

want it makes it easier to identify what you do want. Doing business with the wrong clients can drain your resources such as time, money, staff, and your energy. Choose wisely and avoid desperation selling.

47. ***Thou shall never overindulge.*** Did you know you can talk yourself completely out of a sale? Talking too much in a sales presentation can cause confusion, distrust, feelings of being overwhelmed, or simply take up so much time that there is none left for your prospect to sign up for your offer. ASK QUESTIONS and let the client lead the sales conversation. Learn to not be so anxious and afraid of the BIG FAT Scary NO that you ramble yourself in circles, vomiting information all over the potential client. A sales presentation should be structured and flexible. Disclose information the client is requesting or that could help them with any misunderstandings they need clarification on. Everything doesn't need to be dumped into the clients lap all at once. Avoid information overload and you will close more sales.

48. ***Thou shall start high.*** When positioning offers to potential clients always start high, and then go low. This may cause some of you to shake in your boots, but do it anyways. The human psychology will work for you if you do this. This concept plays

off of the first impression technique. You are setting an anchor for the client to see the most valuable product or service you offer. The top 20% of potential clients you show the higher end offer too will probably accept, the rest will most likely fall into the second or third category of offers. When consumers see more expensive options initially, and then are shown a lower price point they are more willing to accept the secondary offer as it appears much less expensive relative to the higher price. However, if clients are shown a lower price initially then a higher price, the same factors apply and they will deem the higher price as much more expensive relative to the initial lower price offered. Just go for the gusto when offering your products or services and don't try to count other people's money. The client will let you know which option makes the most sense for their needs and budget.

49. ***Thou shall not talk money.*** Have you ever been to a restaurant and wanted to get a substitution or add an additional item and the waiter blurted out, "That will be an additional $2.75". Did this irritate you? Did this make you feel like they were counting your bill or presumed you couldn't afford the extra biscuits? Novice sales people are guilty for this unforgivable habit. If the client doesn't want to talk money yet – then why are you in a

hurry to do so? Allow clients to gather all of the supporting information they need to investigate our product or service first. If you have propositioned your value well enough they will naturally begin the questioning the cost as the next step in the buying cycle. Jumping straight into the price discussion can appear to be desperate, insensitive, and can be quite offensive. If you haven't answered all of the questions and concerns a potential client has about your product or service, then you do not deserve to discuss price tags.

50. *Thou shall incorporate the close early.* Always make it a habit to explain the benefits of your offer several times throughout your consultation and not save it for the end. This sales process works best when you are offering service orientated businesses because as you are working with the client you can physically show them the benefits of your offer throughout the service. Step by step the client is coming to a closing decision as they are experiencing what you are offering through your strategic demonstration and explanation. No one wants to be blindsided by your laundry list of benefits and features at the end of a service and then be expected to make a decision. Illustrate throughout the service and the consultation the offer and then

talk through each benefit with the client as it presents itself in your consultation.

51. ***Thou shall have confidence.*** You are the packaging of the offer. If that packaging isn't solid, then all of the contents are questionable. If you attempt to make a sale and lack confidence your potential client will see that and you will be at risk of being eaten alive by the, "I'll have to think about it" defense. Focus on the value of the product and service you offer and be passionate about your belief that it will be a great investment for the potential client. Stop focusing on the possibility you could be told no. The lack of confidence comes from fear. Fear of rejection is a powerful thing if you lend it focus. Be shameless in sales and allow confidence to be your stability from any rebuttal or rejection you may get. Confidence appears as your unrelenting belief in what you are selling and that alone can be all you need to close the deal.

CHAPTER FIVE

Commandments of Sound Finances

52. ***Thou shall have a Cash Flow Sheet.*** A Cash flow sheet is often never provided to business owners as a part of their monthly and quarterly financials, but it should be. The Cash flow sheet will tell you the truth behind your company's misleading profit and loss and help you hone in on what percentage of sales your expenses are eating up. This provides even the most novices of business owners with clearer vision into their business financial health and gives you the control to adjust the levels of spending in various areas.

53. ***Thou shall invest back into the business.*** As one puts gas in a car for more mileage if you plan to go far in business you better refuel all that has been spent thus far on the journey. Building a business is like building a house. Once you purchase a home, even if it is brand new you eventually will begin making upgrades that will increase the value. Be sure to use a portion of

your business income to upgrade areas in your business. Areas such as advanced technology, a cozier waiting area, adding more client amenities all can add incredible value to your clients' experiences and increase your value – which will allow you to charge more.

54. ***Thou shall pay yourself first out of the profit earned from your toil.*** Do not negate this principle as you will have nothing left to give when the time of growth comes to your door to collect payment. As your business grows you will have more opportunity afforded to you to partner, expand your company, or to be able to afford higher level talent. Many other investment opportunities will appear as you grow that will help you get to the next level if you are positioned to take advantage of them. If you have never mandated of yourself to pay yourself first you will have nothing to give when bigger opportunities present themselves. Don't be a contributor in stunting your own company's growth. Take reinvesting back into yourself as a priority that is non-negotiable. Open up a separate account and have the 10% of revenue automatically sent to this fund.

55. ***Thou shall always know your numbers.*** What you measure you manage. It is human nature to either over estimate or under estimate our progress. Almost next to never are we ever accurate

on how well we really are doing, but numbers do not lie. If you are not familiar with your conversion rates, traffic counts, or your key qualifying data to guide you as to whether or not you are truly winning you are in big trouble. You literally could be going down the wrong path and self-destructing. Measure your company vitals so that your actions and results tell you the real story and it's not just a feeling you have about your success. Be accurate in how well you are doing with a numerical checks and balances system. This system is for you to understand so do not get bogged down with big excel terminology and data sheets in which you don't track because you don't know how to use these resources. Your numbers are your life. By any means necessary, even if it is a notepad – allow your progress to be tracked and measured regularly with numbers – not emotions.

56. ***Thou shall not live the good life too soon.*** There is nothing like opening up your own company and being cheered on by all the local hype men and women who aren't bold enough to take those same steps. Welcome to entrepreneurship, where everyone says you are thriving. You will now be the go to for conversation at any time of the day, because people think you can work when you want and breaks are unlimited. You will also now be the investor into close friends and family member's dreams after the

first few public testimonies you give on your success. In their eyes you are on the door step of becoming a millionaire. Your job is to not allow their praise and the pressure to act like a BIG DOG too fast and too soon to inflate your ego and put you out of business. There is no need to rush to impress those around you. Keep a level head on your finances and time and stay focused when you are new in business. Don't start booking vacations and signing leases for cars and homes just yet. Allow your business to simmer in profitability without ravishing through your company crops too soon. Harvest your success at the right time as pulling up the planted crops too soon will put you back at ground zero.

57. ***Thou shall store up for skinny times.*** With business many unexpected things can pop up at any time and threaten your foundation. Unexpected tax laws, regulations, natural disasters, or even growth. Living pay check to pay check in business and cashing in on every red cent of the profit margin for your personal pleasure is not exactly taking calculated risk. It requires discipline to see a healthy profit margin and not spend it all. Think about your future and protect it.

58. ***Thou shall invest wisely.*** With the money set aside from your earnings make sure you use it only on what you know. Don't

gamble away your financial freedom spending on business ventures you know nothing about. Investing in business ventures you have not researched is like taking out all the money in your bank and allowing the wind to sweep it away as it sees fit. When you plant your seed make sure you investigate the soil. Get prudent guidance in all investments and drink from more than one source of information to find the foundational message. There is safety in council. It is okay to take risks, but make sure they are calculated.

59. ***Thou shall practice resourcefulness.*** It is not always about obtaining what you don't have, but more about making the most out of what you already possess. Resourcefulness can truly create a thriving business. Allowing your creative mind to find more than one usage for tools you use in your company, and even uncovering potential revenue streams in your business can spiral you further than having unlimited access to business capital. Don't despise the days of small beginnings in business because they teach you to use what you have so that it can become more. Lack can be the best teacher you will ever have and abundance can be a crippling disabler.

60. ***Thou shall borrow to grow and not to glow.*** Borrowing should be like pulling back a sling shot, over extending the rubber band

until it can't go anymore and is getting ready to snap, then firing it straight away to propel the ball in a victorious release sending it sailing into unimaginable heights into the sky. Go into debt only if it will get you the tools you need to go further faster. When you borrow capital or other resources they should be spent on forward moving investments. For example, taking out a loan to do more marketing – verses taking out a loan to go on a leisure vacation have two very different outcomes. When a farmer creates a deficit in the soil, they do so to plant a seed that will fill up the hole. Borrowing money isn't a bad practice, unless you don't have a growth plan for the money.

CHAPTER SIX

Commandments of Effortless Operations

61. ***Thou shall not have "shiny object syndrome".*** Invent less and improve more. The shiny object syndrome is one of the biggest enemies to entrepreneurs. Forsaking the work you have already put in, the time you will never get back to go start something totally new, that often times you are not very well versed in. Working on a business, even when it doesn't seem like it is working for you can be very disheartening and make you want to move along to what seems to be taking off like wild fire. Resist the urge when you feel like this. Notice, the word usage - *feel*. Our feelings can get in the way of us operating our businesses with structure and focus. Unless you have hard numbers, measurable data that proves your operations are not working and it is time to move on, just keep perfecting and mastering your already completed business model little by little until you see the results you want.

62. ***Thou shall set your standards.*** When structuring your business it is important to have a definitive understanding of what operational procedures you will conduct and those you will not. For example, will your company need to have quarterly meetings or weekly meetings? Will you need to have audits annually or daily? Will you bring in vendors or will you take on being your own supplier?

63. Create a list at the phase of business you are in now with actionable operations that will only contribute to the health and growth of your company and operational tasks that will distract from the health and growth of your company. Keep in mind that this list will change as the company grows, so be sure to revisit this list and alter your structure regularly. Standards allow you to gain clarity in the overall operations of your business and provide smoother operations because you will limit time wasted on frivolous tasks that don't move your company forward in leaps and bounds.

64. ***Thou shall have checklists.*** Checklists are quick and convenient ways to bring you and your entire organization back to center. Big company manuals mostly are good as dust collectors or to appease the top 20% highly coveted over achievers in the company who read the manuals for leisure. Checklists are quick

ways to check in with your team and your systems to make sure you are hitting all critical areas of your processes. It is similar to when you may pull out that seasonal holiday recipe and overall remember the steps, but feel like you might be missing one or two important items of the process. Don't skip a beat in keeping your organization running, and don't soak up too much time building a 20 pound manual that will hardly be used. Keep your operations running smoothly with easy to read and easy to remember checklists for every department in your organization.

65. ***Thou shall divorce your plans.*** Plans are wonderful until they don't work. Don't marry your business plans and particularly your operations. Be able to let go of the old ways of doing things to discover an easier and more efficient process. This is where a little ego deflating may take place, but it is truly for the betterment of your company. Be open to redefining a broken or inefficient process to help the end user and those you hire to serve your company. Check in with your systems and procedures regularly and look for opportunities to improve them, then do not be afraid to walk away from what use to work.

66. ***Thou shall request team feedback.*** Your operational team and their feedback are super important when running an organization. Have you ever worked at a normal 9-5 before

stepping out as an entrepreneur and had the big guy in the corporation put out a new procedure and thought to yourself, What is this guy thinking? The number one reason you thought this is because you knew these orders were coming from someone who clearly did not actually perform the processes they were changing. You probably thought, I wish they'd ask me. Getting feedback is like having eyes in the back of your head. The more feedback you can get from your team about your operations the better. You will be able to discover common likes and dislikes and investigate more clearly into what you really should change in the organization. Requesting feedback from your team will also allow them to know they have a voice and you as their leader care about their job duties.

67. ***Thou shall be an observer.*** Watch your operations regularly to audit the levels of effectiveness. Observe the processes and procedures in action and look for loopholes, inefficiencies, or money saving opportunities. Don't just allow your team to tell you how they perform their jobs; observe the processes live and in person. This is so important they made a show out if it! If you have ever seen Undercover Boss, that show rests on this key principle. You have to actually see to believe your own operations. While creating and innovating is important,

checking in with your existing foundation is very vital to ensure you are not adding new processes on top of crumbling foundations.

68. ***Thou shall have an audit system.*** Measurement of numbers keeps you on track and aware of any out of place activities. Businesses have a lot of moving parts, deadlines, and laws they must abide by. Creating an internal audit that can be conducted monthly, semi-annually, and annually will keep you and your staff in line with ensuring you are following all of the governing rules of your organization. The audit should be performed by the key people in your organization who have a natural talent for attention to detail, recorded, and retained as ongoing records. If you reach that point of selling your company and you have a long track record of internal audits to handover you will increase the value of your asset more, because you have proven that you lowered the risk in your business operations through internal controls.

69. ***Thou shall have visible signage.*** If you want to make sure your entire staff in on the same page, then you must post cues for them to follow throughout your organization. Information out of sight is out of mind. Slip paging the latest monthly promotion in your company's 350 page manual will be a sure

way to ensure it never gets read. Sending emails, text messages, and videos to your staff are all helpful, but the messages are easily forgotten when your staff has returned to their normal work areas and day to day functionalities. If you want something to be remembered, then remind them. Make the message plain and obvious where your staff frequents the most so that you can communicate important messages of success. Even if you do not have a staff, keeping memos and important tools within your sight and range will help you acknowledge them more as well.

70. ***Thou shall secure your treasures.*** Security is a vital part of world class customer service and excellent leadership. Although not obviously connected, whether conducting all business over the internet or meeting with clients face to face when you protect them and their information you have served one of their six basic human needs – the need to feel secure. Being able to secure your operations demonstrates that you care about your organization and the people in it. Consider how many organizations faced damnation when their internal records were breached or there was a physical attack on staff members. The whole company was ripped apart in an investigation of their security measures which were in place at the time that possibly could have prevented the occurrence. Security is like insurance

that you create for your clients and your staff. It allows you to be proactive verses reactive. Holding security trainings and checking to make sure security measures are being followed at all times will help your company avoid pitfalls from the evil that lurks around unassuming businesses.

71. *Thou shall not be imprisoned by operations.* Operations in a company are guidelines, not indefinite truths. Being unwilling to budge from protocol can sacrifice your mission of world class client service. Sometimes exceptions will need to be made in your organization for the bigger picture. If you have an operational guideline that is preventing the right people from doing business with you or that is threatening a long term client relationship, by not considering a work around you could be doing more harm than if you would have just bent the rule. Each situation in rule bending will be unique, but you must learn to set the proper authority levels in your company for exceptions that can be made. Train your staff to make executive decisions and help them understand the reasoning behind rule bending. There is no black and white in businesses that serve others. One offs are a part of the process and sometimes exceptions, that do not violate the company's risk management guidelines should

be made. Going outside of your operation standards to satisfy a great client is called taking a calculated risk.

72. ***Thou shall outsource.*** Third party relationships in a growing organization are a great thing if chosen wisely. By hiring a company or vendor to help you with a piece of your operations you can save capital for your bottom line. Rather than spending countless time recruiting, interviewing, vetting, hiring, training, and cultivating one person on an area of your business, there are many companies out there now that can service that same function in your organization with a team of experts at half the cost. Take a look at your organization and consider what can be outsourced and what affects outsourcing that component may have on your business. Will it affect your clients or is it an internal procedure, can your company grow with delegating that component to outsourcing, or will you eventually have to bring that component back in house once you hit a certain level of growth? Outsourcing can certainly save you time and money and be a great way to speed up organizational growth. Outsourcing can allow small businesses to function like major corporations. There are some companies where you can hire highly skilled CFOs for your organization for a monthly fee,

once it makes sense for you to do so. You don't have to actually be big to operate big, but you do have to think big.

CHAPTER SEVEN

Commandments of a Success Mindset

73. ***Thou shall time block your schedule.*** Time block your schedule so that you will not be like a weightless feather tossed in the wind easily pushed around floating from task to task. Set aside blocks of time to dedicate your full attention to one single task at hand until the period of time has elapsed. This focused time is a key element of success that will allow you to use concentrated energy and execute tasks much quicker. Choose about 3-5 periods of time blocks, ranging from 90 minutes to 2 hours per day with a 15 – 30 minute rest between each period. At the end of the designated time, whether the task is completed or not – stop and go one to the next time block.

74. ***Thou shall know your mission statement.*** What good is it for a man to plot his course, pack all his belongings, bid his family and friends' good bye, burn his boats, then forget where he was headed and why? Your mission statement will guide everything

you do in your business. It will allow you to drive your business boat with clarity and certainty. With a mission statement you will be able to strategically decipher if a task or business relationship is worth your time and prevent being overwhelmed with details that don't address your ultimate goal in your mission. Why are you *really* doing this business? What do you *truly* want to gain from it? Questions like this will allow you to set your boundaries in business and lessen some of the stresses that accompany confusion.

75. **Thou shall fail.** If you have been in business any amount of time you have probably heard that failure is a great thing. Scary huh? No one wants to fail, even though they say it is good for us. Being told to accept failure as a good thing is like being a 9 year old kid served raw broccoli and cooked liver for dinner and being told to eat it because it will make you stronger. We don't want that plate! Failure doesn't exactly taste good no matter how good it is for us. The key to failure is not just to accept that it exists, but to add a little flavor to the situation with the frame of attitude and proper understanding of the lesson it teaches. There are so many valuable lessons to be learned in our own failures, as well as those around us which guide us away from the wrong doors to the right ones. Keep moving forward to experience the

benefits of failure. If you wallow in it then failure will never do you any good, add your own flavor to the circumstance, swallow it down, and let it nourish the strength of your business and entrepreneurship skill sets.

76. *Thou shall gain new wisdom daily.* Make learning an everyday occurrence. As the good old saying in business pronounces, "Shift happens". Businesses evolve daily, and you cannot operate on stale knowledge. Make it a habit to read daily, like millionaires do, about something that will grow your business. Don't just read to say you can check the task off, but read to understand, to learn something new, and seek to implement something you have read from the literary source within that week. Reading enhances creativity and it is the creativity in which success is born.

77. *Thou shall maintain an updated vision board.* If you are thinking vision boards are for hocus pocus belief and just a wish to success, than you have not capitalized on one of the key secrets of business success. As a true leader in business your number one objective is to SEE something those you lead and those you sell to overlook. You literally create something from nothing and envision an idea until it manifests into a physical reality. You allow your thoughts and imagination to grow legs

and arms and develop into an "I told you so" invention that is useable and helpful. A vision board is simply a blue print of what you believe. A human brain processes 600 million bits of VISUAL information in just one minute. When you allow yourself to see the reality you strive to create your brain takes it in as truth. Your brain is the communication center for your emotions and actions and will drive you to manifest those visual cues. Vision boards are very influential to your thought processes, your emotional health, and your hope as entrepreneurs when things don't always go your way. Do not skimp on the chance to write out the vision and make it plain so that you may be reminded of the success that lies in wait for you.

78. ***Thou shall be conscious of the subconscious.*** This is very important because business owners operate in a realm of thinking that many others may not. Your mental aptitude is so critical to how you perform in business and being pessimistic will kill your chances of success in the business world. One of the best things any entrepreneur can learn is how to control what their subconscious mind is subjected to by taking great care of their conscious thoughts. All success is originated from our ideas. It is the ability to manifest that success that comes

from our beliefs. You are much more powerful in business when you are aware of your deeply rooted thought processes and face limiting beliefs head on. A lot of how and why we as humans take, or avoid taking certain actions is directly related to what we believe internally. The more in tune you are with your internal belief system and strive to spend time developing your self-awareness the better you will be in manifesting the business success you seek.

79. ***Thou shall fall madly in love with self-development.*** As the core processor for the business you have created you must make it a priority to stay as healthy and conditioned as possible. From your mental health to your physical health – both are very important factors that will dictate how far your idea for business can go. Spend daily moments in self-development. Work out daily, meditate, journal, read self-help literary works, say positive affirmations, pray, spend time with those you love, and do whatever will help cultivate you. If you will not spend time investing in yourself, why would someone else want to invest in you?

80. ***Thou shall be happy now.*** Do not fall into the trap of believing you will be happy once you become successful. You will be chasing a feeling that you will never catch because as soon as you

obtain the goal, you will set a new goal and base happiness on obtaining that one. Find happiness in where you are right now and with what you are becoming. Learn to enjoy the journey along the way which is truly your freedom.

81. ***Thou shall stay uncomfortable.*** Have you ever found yourself in that perfect snug position on the couch, cuddled up in a warm blanket, feet up, head propped on a nicely fluffed pillow, where you were watching your favorite show and then the tinkle monster creeps in and you have to use the restroom? Did your brain go into instant debate as to whether or not you really needed to go or if you could hold it for another 2 hours to finish your movie? You probably started to think about how badly you didn't feel like moving from your spot and delayed taking care of your natural needs as long as you could - willing to sacrifice your bladder to remain comfortable. Comfort stops the process of us doing tasks that must be completed to stay healthy in business. We will procrastinate even if it may have damaging effects on our vital organizational functions. We may overlook how important it is to take certain actions now and cause us to be a step behind in progress because we didn't want to have our comforts interrupted. Don't get trapped in comfort. When business is doing well and you can let up off the throttle a little,

always be disciplined enough to move at any moment. When comfort kicks in so does idleness. Idleness is the killer of growth and innovation. No great thing ever emerged from comfort.

82. ***Thou shall test limits daily.*** Business is a muscle. In order to grow muscles you have to overstretch them, breaking them down so that they can be rebuilt to be stronger. Staying within the realms you normally operate in is complacency. Find one thing, no matter how big or small to push just a little harder each day. Do something out of your comfort zone and stay risk tolerant by continuously subjecting yourself to opportunities for growth. Read something at a higher level, study a different marketing angle, and interact with someone smarter or more successful than yourself, run that extra mile – literally.

83. ***Thou shall be stingy with your schedule.*** Time is something you will never get back. How you use your time is what separates you from success and failure. Remember there is no *free time*. All time costs you something in your life bank. Either you are spending your time on forward moving activities or you are wasting your time on things that will not optimize your future success. When you think about time as you do money it may allow you to understand why it is so valuable. The key difference however, between money and time, is money you can get back,

but time you cannot. Refrain from allowing tasks, habits, people, and activities that have little to no value drain your time bank. Invest your time in only forward moving opportunities in every area of your life. If it is productive to your future self, then spend your time there.

84. ***Thou shall work consistently.*** It isn't about the sprint as much as it is about the endurance. Many people can have a fight or flight reaction to success. Maybe they get highly motivated after going to a seminar or taking a dip in their cash flows so they do enough to get a little further and then they start feeling the rays of success on their skin and slack off. Maybe someone took off in a sprint so fast and hard because they thought the finish line was closer than it actually was and they ran out of steam on the first lap. Understand that business is a marathon, not a sprint and it takes a lot of lung capacity and proper pacing to make it to the end. You may not go as fast as others initially, but as long as you don't stop like they probably will you will finish first. Your steady pace will make up for their rest periods. The race is truly not given to the swift or to the strong but to him that endures.

85. ***Thou shall acquire mentors the right way.*** Mentors are a key part of your development as an entrepreneur. With the right

mentor you can discover areas of your talent that can catapult you into a level of success you never dreamed possible. This is why mentors are so important and so frequently sought out by new business owners. The thing to remember however is mentors like to be in control of who their mentees are. When acquiring a mentor do so in an ethical way. Do not try to become an imposter and infiltrate their inner circle to only steal the droppings of their knowledge. Simply put, ask and don't take. Don't get offended either if the desired mentor tells you no. Remember, all successful people are very careful with their time and will often say no to an opportunity that they are not able to give their full attention to. Keep doing what you can do to further develop yourself, and keep asking the mentor for the opportunity to learn from them. Be sure you treat your desired mentor with respect and do not ask empty handed. The absolute worse way to try to acquire a mentor is to try and position yourself in their network and copycat everything they do, then go out and try to do it on your own as a competitor. This is not true desire to be mentored, but is selfish desire to get to the top the easy way. A mentor will educate you in principals and foundational business truths that allow you the freedom to choose the method. They will send you through hard lessons and put you in extreme discomfort to grow your value. Be sure you seek out the right mentor who has values you stand behind.

86. ***Thou shall always have at least 3 options before making a decision.*** Making a decision with only one option is for the desperate, making a decision with two options is for the risky, making a decision with three or more options is for the prudent. Be sure that you allow you're the opportunity to have more than one option in all business decisions you must make. Each decision made in business contributes to the ultimate destination of your company. One decision can crush all you have worked for, and one decision can show you the red carpet to success. Weigh each option presented before you with prudence and timely investigation of the outcome. All options may not be made equal, but one is certain to be attached to the greater good of your company.

87. ***Thou shall read daily.*** Constant knowledge acquisition is the only key to business survival. Industries change daily and without notice and if your wisdom is outdated so will be your business. Reading things about your industry, trends, up and coming markets, the history of your industry and the future are all great indicators for you on how to plan your course of action. Reading keeps you plugged into the source and fresh of ideas.

Ideas have power to move you forward. Stay tuned in to your industry by digesting as much literature as possible on a consistent basis. Plan to read every day for at least 15 minutes.

88. ***Thou shall work out daily.*** Physical strength is the defining factor of how well you are able to apply yourself mentally to your business. Being ill can serve as a major distraction or bring a halt to your entire business operations. Take care of your health with active lifestyle choices daily. Don't allow your business to be an excuse to die a slow death. As you plan your budget and marketing take time to plan for your health. Working out delivers more than just good looks, which are also a very helpful tool in business; but it also supports healthy blood flow and increases oxygen throughout your body decreasing stress and encouraging clarity of mind. Take care of yourself first or you won't be around to take care of your business.

89. ***Thou shall have positive affirmations.*** Speak to yourself as you would to others with faith, hope, and love. We can be our worse critic and being hard on ourselves is often why most businesses never get off the ground in the first place. We talk ourselves out of so many great opportunities because we look at who we were in the past or what we currently have to offer now. Affirmations are about whom you are capable of being in the future by

claiming it in the now. Life and death are in the power of the tongue and your word choices can talk up a very positive future. The wonderful thing about affirmations is you don't have to feel like they are true statements in the here and now, but you have to firmly believe that they will happen for you because you are committing to work for them.

90. ***Thou shall write down your vision.*** Writing has so much confirmation to our desires. Thoughts can be fleeting, but the writing down of your vision makes it plain. Writing is almost like repeating our thoughts out loud, but instead we reflect our thoughts back to us with what we see in our own writings. Write out the vision to plan, to create, to solidify your wants as a declaration of truth in your life. Make it a habit to read your thoughts aloud and reflect on the vision you were given. Ingest your future on a daily basis.

91. ***Thou shall not quit challenges.*** Saying running a business will get hard at some point and then actually enduring the harsh moments are two different things. As entrepreneurs you are constantly being warned about the dangers ahead that face you and you are obviously optimistic or you wouldn't have even begun the journey, but hold fast when you actually do face turmoil. The challenges truly do come to make you stronger.

Without challenges we would operate in complacency and do things as we always have done them. Challenges are simply opportunities to go higher. Challenges can also be opportunities to redirect. Are there times where quitting is permissible? Yes. There are times when quitting is absolutely necessary and it all depends on what outcome you are after that will justify waiving the white flag. Selling or closing a business that is in a dying industry is a great reason to quite, but closing up a business because you can't figure out how to make sales like your competitors isn't. Allow challenges to stretch you and learn from each one. The trouble lies when we don't heed the lessons and keep going.

92. *Thou shall express gratitude daily.* Don't let your goals consume your smile. Entrepreneurs are by nature highly charged goal chasers and forward thinking people. Many have a hard time being satisfied with the conditions right now. There is this whisper in your mind that says "I can't wait till we gross XXXX in revenues!" or "I'll be so happy when I finally land this deal!" but what about right now? What are you doing well at this very present moment? What can you be proud of today? Goals and gratitude can conflict. You are hyper focused on where you want to be that you forget where you are. It is however in the

appreciation of where you are today that you will find your tomorrow. Always looking ahead at what hasn't happened yet can be a bit of a confidence bummer because you are looking at what you haven't yet become. Looking at what you have accomplished today with gratitude can be a confidence booster because you see that you have actually achieved something. Allow those two to work hand in hand for your good. Don't be so focused on the future you lose your footing in the now. Practice gratitude every day for where you have come from letting that fuel your confidence for where you are going.

93. *Thou shall revisit why.* Why ask why? Why means; for what reason or purpose. For what reason or purpose did you begin your company? For what reason or purpose are you still running your company? For what reason or purpose do you hope to contribute to? Revisiting your company's reason or purpose narrows the target. You avoid pitfalls and side tracks because you keep your reasoning for what you are doing front and center. Your why can also evolve and probably should as you grow. Through growth in business you will find that some things you thought aren't actually what they seemed and at certain phases you will reposition your reasoning for doing business to better

fit where you are at that moment. Knowing your why is how to begin with the end in mind.

94. ***Thou shall not be intimidated to ask for help.*** Asking for help by far can be one of the biggest pitfalls of entrepreneurs. Either we do not trust other people, we doubt their abilities, or we feel like we can't afford help so we don't even bother to ask. We forget that many people admire business owners and are willing to lend a hand to see the company flourish. You cannot do it all. When you refuse to get help you are positioning yourself to be a jack of all trades and a master of none. This leads to mediocre success. The specialists get all the prestige. By not asking for help you are at risk for burn out, organizational neglect, and failure. As you grow you should be looking for tasks that you can assign to someone else so that more of your time can be spent on what you are the expert at. Asking for help from others also benefits them. People have a strong desire to matter and to be a part of something bigger than them. When someone who is trustworthy and able to perform the task wants to help – don't be too proud to accept it.

95. ***Thou shall say NO (a lot).*** When people say they are overwhelmed they are saying they do not feel in control. When people become entrepreneurs it is primarily to gain more control

over their lives or a situation. When you find yourself feeling overwhelmed as an entrepreneur it will feel like failure because you feel like you are not in control. One sure way to avoid this – JUST SAY NO. Say no to sales pitches that come to take away from your profitability, say no to time wasters that come to rob you of productivity, say no to negative conversations that drain your happiness, say no to calls that interrupt your day and creative thought processes, say no to dinner meetings just to appease someone else, say no to marketing campaigns you don't believe in, say no to charities that you aren't totally in support of, just learn to say no. Two things that will completely free anyone whether in business or not –the art of not caring what others think about you and the art of saying no.

96. ***Thou shall keep a journal of thoughts.*** Write down your inner conversations and express it in a keepsake. Journaling is developmental therapy. Therapy is something you need a lot of with the never ending thought cycle as an entrepreneur. A private record of thoughts, insecurities, struggles, achievements, frustrations, and hopes where no one can judge or question you will be your freedom. Don't worry about correct grammar or punctuation, just dump your cares, worries, and happiness through the ink, or keyboard if you are technical and relieve

your mind of the burden to try and carry it all. Journaling will also give birth to brainstorming new ideas and concepts that may be the key to the next level of success for you. All multi-million dollar businesses began with one single idea. Never skimp on the opportunity to spend time lightening your load and sharpening your mind.

97. *Thou shall break bread with the wise.* Eat with people smarter than you so you can educate your pallet. Ego doesn't belong in business because it is like a chain that will keep you enslaved. When you are willing to subject yourself in discomfort to be around more powerful business owners whose levels of wisdom and experience make yours a joke you will inherently reap the benefits from their presence. Humble yourself to spend time where you are stretched and tried. Go get beat up in a business meeting with more prominent and wise people than yourself and you will find that you become better at your goals. Strength is never born out of comfort.

98. *Thou shall watch the company you keep.* Your circle of influence is more vital than you may be aware of. It has long been communicated to us that we are the product of the 5 closest people we interact with. There are many things to pay attention to when you are sharing your time, space, and intimate

information with people. Taking a look at their lives is important, because you must have someone who can inspire you in return. Relationships are like life cycles and if even the earth and the sky give back to one another than why shouldn't those who you keep in your company be tasked with the same. Be aware of takers who only come to get all they can gain and move onto another source of energy. Be very selective with those you allow to consume your time and intellect.

99. ***Thou shall spend time in reflection.*** Taking time out in solitude is the best medicine. Entrepreneurs should be incredibly stingy with their personal reflection time. Since you are the brains of your operations mental exhaustion can take place much more quickly in your life than those who do not carry as much responsibility as you do. Be very stingy with stealing away moments of solidarity where there are no phones, televisions, white noise, family, or friends. Reflect on who you are and all you have done. Life as an entrepreneur moves at a fast pace always working upstream and will drown you if not managed with care. Demand personal reflection time from your busy schedule for at least 15 minutes daily and your company's success and personal health will reward you for it.

100. ***Thou shall give your 10%.*** Did you know that you can distance yourself from those in your industry positioning yourself as an expert if you do just 10% more than those around you? Yes – just 10% more. Where many get discouraged is they think you beat out the competition by leaps and bounds, but a really small habit done consistently is how you gain maximum results. Compound your efforts and don't stop at good enough. Stay later, show up earlier, write more, study harder, go the extra mile.

101. ***Thou shall finish.*** Done is better than great. In a quest to become the BEST, the NEWEST, the GREATEST we sometimes become the non-existent. We want what we put out to be perfection and while that is a great goal, sometimes…well most of the times actually completing a task that you tried your best at is more important than it being perfect. Don't procrastinate moving forward with action because you are seeking to be perfect. Once an idea is thought of the most important part of the process is implementation and action, and trial and error will build the rest. Give yourself a break, forgive yourself for mistakes that you will make in the future, and publish your ideas knowing they are works in progress.

An ending thought from the author:

Thank you for taking your success as an entrepreneur seriously. By investing in yourself, you automatically invest in your company and those around you. Always remember to be a continuous learner and to never get full of wisdom. The more valuable you become the more value you can give others. Wisdom is your weapon in business, so keep it sharp.

www.ingramcontent.com/pod-product-compliance
Lightning Source LLC
Chambersburg PA
CBHW030450220526
45464CB00006B/2467